The MISEDUCATION of the Negro in the 21st Century

College/University Teacher's Edition by Cedric A. Washington

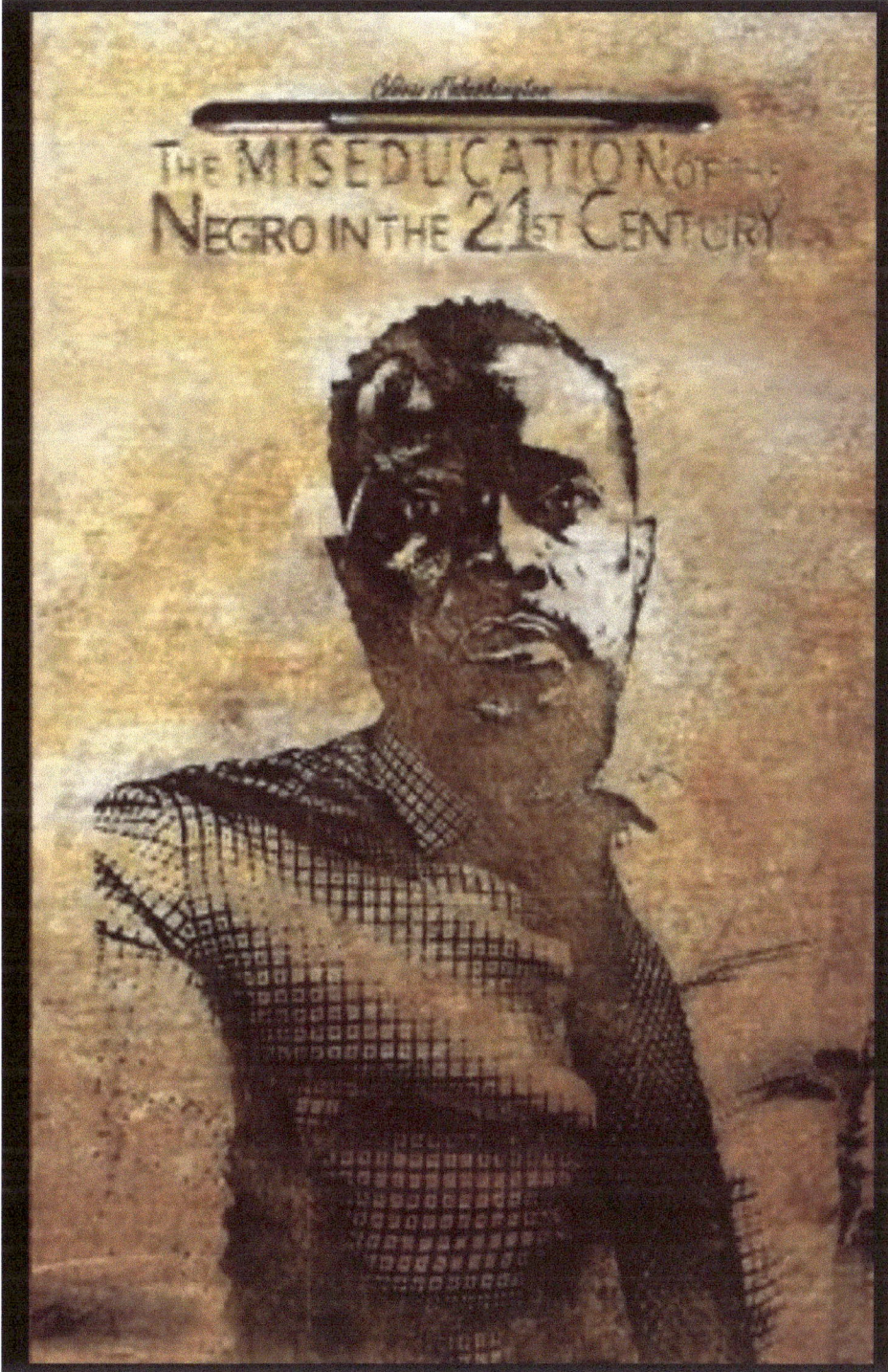

Table of Contents

Dedication

This work is dedicated to every young mind determined to break free from the chains of miseducation. To the students who question, the teachers who empower, and the ancestors whose sacrifices paved the road we walk today.

May this guide serve as a light, a weapon, and a foundation.
Never forget — you were born to lead, not follow.
The world is your classroom. The truth is your legacy.

- Cedric A. Washington
Author. Educator. Revolutionary.

The MISEDUCATION of the Negro in the 21st Century – College/University Teacher's Edition

Who Lives Like This?! Publishing LLC
www.nerdyouthservices.org

ISBN: 978-1-970680-06-5 (Hardback)

Cover design and interior layout by
Who Lives Like This?! Publishing LLC Design Team

Printed in the United States of America

First Edition — 2025

THE MISEDUCATION OF THE NEGRO

IN THE 21ST CENTURY

COLLEGE / UNIVERSITY / PROFESSOR'S EDITION

Teach Like Ced™ Series
Knowledge of S.E.L.F. (Social Empowerment Learning Framework)
By **Cedric A. Washington**

PREFACE — PROFESSOR'S EDITION

(Foundational Text for Seminar Instruction)

I. POSITIONING THE PREFACE (FOR FACULTY)

The Preface is not introductory commentary.
It is the **thesis declaration** of the entire work.

Cedric A. Washington establishes, from the outset, that the problem is not student failure, teacher incompetence, or community deficiency, but **systemic miseducation**—a process that suppresses culture, punishes authenticity, and prioritizes compliance over intelligence.

At the collegiate level, this Preface functions as:

- a **primary text**
- a **counter-narrative to institutional pedagogy**
- a **framework for interrogating education as power**

This Preface should be taught **before** any attempt to contextualize chapters historically, politically, or theologically.

II. CORE CLAIMS EMERGING FROM THE PREFACE

(Text-Derived — No Interpretation Added)

From the author's own language, the Preface asserts:

1. Education systems can **stifle the pedagogy of effective teachers**
2. State standards often override **cultural competency**
3. Urban education requires **improvisation under scarcity**
4. Data-driven discipline prioritizes documentation over humanity
5. Compliance is mistaken for professionalism
6. Teaching in ways that contradict internal knowledge is **intellectual slavery**
7. True intelligence emerges from **culture and lived experience**
8. Knowledge of S.E.L.F. is a corrective force against miseducation

These claims are not hypothetical.
They are drawn directly from lived professional experience.

III. PREFACE AS A COLLEGIATE TEXT

At the university level, students should be taught to read this Preface as:

- an **institutional critique**
- a **professional autobiography**
- a **pedagogical manifesto**
- a **cultural indictment**
- a **call to intellectual courage**

This text does not ask for agreement.
It demands **engagement**.

IV. SEMINAR ENTRY QUESTIONS (TEXT-ANCHORED)

These questions are designed for **graduate- and undergraduate-level discourse**.

1. How does the author distinguish between education and knowledge in practice?
2. What does it mean for pedagogy to be "natural" versus "compliant"?
3. Why does the author reject data-driven discipline models?

4. In what ways does the Preface redefine professionalism in education?
5. How does the author's firing function as evidence rather than failure?
6. What is meant by "turning water into Hennessey" in institutional contexts?
7. Why does the author frame miseducation as a form of slavery?

Students must cite **specific passages** from the Preface to support responses.

V. INSTRUCTOR FACILITATION NOTES

(University Context)

- Do **not** soften language for student comfort
- Allow productive discomfort
- Resist premature moral conclusions
- Emphasize **systems**, not individuals
- Encourage students to locate themselves within the critique

This text should not be rushed.
The Preface can sustain **1–2 full class sessions**.

VI. WRITING EXPECTATIONS (COLLEGIATE)

Analytical Response (Short Essay)

Prompt:
Using only the Preface, analyze how Cedric A. Washington defines miseducation as a systemic condition rather than an individual failure.

Requirements:

- Text-based evidence
- Academic tone
- No outside sources
- No personal narrative unless text-supported

Reflective Synthesis (Optional)

Prompt:
Where do you see the tension between compliance and intelligence operating in institutions you have experienced?

VII. KNOWLEDGE OF S.E.L.F. — COLLEGIATE ENTRY POINT

The Preface introduces **SELF Conscience** as the foundational domain.

At the university level, SELF Conscience manifests as:

- intellectual honesty
- refusal to compartmentalize truth
- courage to challenge institutional norms
- awareness of one's position within systems

This is not SEL as behavior management.
This is **SEL as consciousness development**.

VIII. WHY THE PREFACE MATTERS AT THIS LEVEL

College is where:

- students are preparing to enter systems
- ideology meets consequence
- theory meets lived reality

The Preface forces students to confront a critical question:

If education requires you to abandon what you know to be true, who does it actually serve?

CHAPTER 1 — PRIVILEGE

(Institutional Access, Power, and Psychological Inheritance)

I. ACADEMIC POSITIONING OF THE CHAPTER (FOR FACULTY)

Chapter 1 establishes **privilege** as the foundational condition that structures every subsequent chapter.
Before leadership, before education, before politics, before culture, **access** determines trajectory.

Cedric A. Washington frames privilege not as individual guilt, but as **systemic inheritance**—embedded in law, policy, schooling, and historical timing.

At the collegiate level, this chapter should be treated as:

- a **historical argument**
- a **structural analysis**
- a **counter-narrative to meritocracy**
- an **entry point into psychological enslavement**

This chapter must be taught **before** any discussion of achievement gaps, leadership failure, or behavior.

II. CORE CLAIMS EMERGING FROM THE TEXT

(Directly Derived from Chapter 1)

From the author's language and sequencing, the chapter asserts:

1. Educational deficit in Black America is **historical and cumulative**
2. Charter school expansion is tied to urban educational displacement
3. Mainstream standards are not culturally neutral
4. Privilege is embedded in constitutional timing
5. Psychological enslavement outlives legal emancipation
6. Liberation requires knowledge of self, not proximity to systems
7. Education without cultural grounding perpetuates domination

These claims are presented as **continuations of Carter G. Woodson's analysis**, not revisions.

III. HISTORICAL ANCHORING (TEXT-FAITHFUL)

Washington grounds privilege historically through:

- the Constitution (1776)
- Emancipation delayed by geography (June 19, 1865)
- Reconstruction-era philosophical responses (Garvey, Washington, Du Bois)
- Psychological aftermath of enslavement

Privilege is therefore not accidental.
It is **timed**, **structured**, and **protected**.

This chapter reframes privilege as **access to the promise of America**, not effort.

IV. SEMINAR QUESTIONS (COLLEGIATE LEVEL)

These questions are designed for **sustained academic dialogue**.

1. How does Washington define privilege beyond economics?
2. Why is the Constitution central to understanding educational privilege?
3. How does delayed emancipation function psychologically?
4. What role does charter school proliferation play in modern miseducation?
5. Why does the author emphasize psychological enslavement over physical bondage?
6. How does this chapter extend Woodson's original thesis?
7. Why must privilege be understood before discussing leadership or behavior?

Students must cite **specific passages** to ground claims.

V. INTERDISCIPLINARY APPLICATION

(Without Adding New Theory)

This chapter operates simultaneously within:

- **Education Studies**: access, curriculum control, schooling structures

- **Sociology**: stratification, inheritance, systemic advantage
- **Political Science**: constitutional timing, legal access
- **African American Studies**: post-emancipation consciousness
- **Psychology**: internalized limitation

The chapter does not ask permission to cross disciplines.
It assumes reality already does.

VI. WRITING & RESEARCH EXPECTATIONS (COLLEGIATE)

Analytical Essay

Prompt:
Using Chapter 1 only, analyze how privilege functions as a system of access rather than an individual advantage.

Requirements:

- Direct textual evidence
- Historical grounding
- No outside theorists
- No anecdotal substitution

Argument Development Task

Prompt:
Explain why Washington insists that miseducation cannot be corrected without first confronting privilege.

VII. INSTRUCTOR FACILITATION NOTES

- Allow discomfort without resolution
- Avoid moralizing privilege
- Emphasize systems over identity
- Recenter discussion when it drifts toward individual blame
- Keep Woodson present as intellectual lineage, not ornament

This chapter may require **multiple sessions**.

VIII. KNOWLEDGE OF S.E.L.F. — COLLEGIATE ALIGNMENT

SELF Conscience is activated here as:

- recognition of inherited position
- awareness of systemic advantage/disadvantage
- refusal to internalize imposed limitation

Privilege is not presented as shame.
It is presented as **context**.

IX. WHY THIS CHAPTER MATTERS AT THE UNIVERSITY LEVEL

Universities often assume:

- students arrive equally prepared
- access equals merit
- opportunity is neutral

This chapter dismantles that assumption **before students enter the workforce**, where privilege operates invisibly.

THE MISEDUCATION OF THE NEGRO

IN THE 21ST CENTURY

COLLEGE / UNIVERSITY / PROFESSOR'S EDITION

CHAPTER 2 — FIGUREHEAD

(Symbolic Leadership, Institutional Obedience, and Controlled Authority)

I. ACADEMIC POSITIONING OF THE CHAPTER (FOR FACULTY)

Chapter 2 interrogates **leadership without power**.

Cedric A. Washington exposes figurehead leadership as one of the most dangerous mechanisms sustaining miseducation because it creates the **illusion of progress while protecting the system**.

At the collegiate level, this chapter must be treated as:

- a **leadership critique**
- an **institutional analysis**
- a **psychological study of compliance**
- a **continuation of enslavement through administration**

This chapter builds directly on **privilege** by revealing what happens when limited access is rewarded with symbolic authority.

II. CORE CLAIMS EMERGING FROM THE TEXT

(Strictly Derived from Chapter 2)

From the author's language and sequencing, the chapter asserts:

1. Figurehead leadership maintains systems rather than challenges them
2. Black principals often operate without real decision-making power
3. Advancement within institutions frequently requires obedience
4. Job security becomes a silencing mechanism
5. Discipline policies are weaponized against Black children
6. Leadership titles mask institutional exploitation
7. Miseducation persists through symbolic representation

Leadership, in this chapter, is framed not as intention—but as **function**.

III. HISTORICAL AND IDEOLOGICAL ANCHORING

Washington grounds this chapter through:

- Carter G. Woodson's warning about miseducated Negro leadership
- Malcolm X's *House Negro vs. Field Negro* analogy
- Modern school governance structures
- The school-to-prison pipeline

Figurehead leadership is shown as **a modern translation of an old control mechanism**.

IV. SEMINAR QUESTIONS (COLLEGIATE LEVEL)

These questions are designed for **sustained, high-level discourse**.

1. How does Washington define a figurehead beyond the dictionary definition?
2. Why does the author focus on Black principals specifically?
3. How does job security function as a form of control?
4. In what ways do discipline policies reproduce enslavement?
5. Why is symbolic representation insufficient for liberation?
6. How does Woodson's critique of miseducated leadership apply here?
7. Why does Washington compare modern administrators to the "house negro"?

Students must cite **specific passages** to support arguments.

V. INSTITUTIONAL ANALYSIS (TEXT-FAITHFUL)

Washington reveals that schools prioritize:

- order over humanity
- data over relationship
- compliance over intelligence
- optics over outcomes

The figurehead is essential to this process because they:

- enforce policies they did not create
- discipline children they understand
- protect institutions that harm their own communities

This is not personal failure.
It is **structural coercion**.

VI. WRITING & RESEARCH EXPECTATIONS (COLLEGIATE)

Analytical Essay

Prompt:
Using Chapter 2 only, analyze how figurehead leadership sustains miseducation within educational institutions.

Requirements:

- Text-based evidence
- System-level analysis
- No anecdotal substitution
- No outside theorists

Position Paper

Prompt:
Explain why Washington argues that representation without power is more dangerous than exclusion.

VII. INSTRUCTOR FACILITATION NOTES

- Do not personalize critique toward individual administrators
- Keep focus on **systems of governance**
- Expect emotional responses—do not suppress them
- Redirect debate toward institutional function
- Reinforce continuity with Chapters 1 and 3

This chapter often provokes **strong reactions**—that tension is pedagogically productive.

VIII. KNOWLEDGE OF S.E.L.F. — COLLEGIATE ALIGNMENT

SELF Governing emerges here as:

- the ability to lead without institutional permission
- the refusal to confuse title with authority
- the courage to challenge systems rather than manage harm

Figurehead leadership is framed as the absence of SELF Governing.

IX. WHY THIS CHAPTER MATTERS AT THE UNIVERSITY LEVEL

Universities frequently celebrate:

- diversity in leadership
- representation in administration
- symbolic inclusion

This chapter forces students to ask:

Who holds power—and who enforces it?

That question is unavoidable in the real world.

THE MISEDUCATION OF THE NEGRO

IN THE 21ST CENTURY

COLLEGE / UNIVERSITY / PROFESSOR'S EDITION

CHAPTER 3 — KNOWLEDGE VS. EDUCATION

(Control of Information, Identity, and Intellectual Power)

I. ACADEMIC POSITIONING OF THE CHAPTER (FOR FACULTY)

Chapter 3 is the **philosophical core** of the text.

Cedric A. Washington does not debate whether education is important.
He interrogates **who controls education**, **what is taught**, and **what is intentionally omitted**.

At the collegiate level, this chapter functions as:

- a **definition war**
- a **critique of institutional authority**
- a **framework for intellectual liberation**
- a **bridge between identity and power**

This chapter must be taught slowly.
It reframes what students believe learning actually is.

II. DEFINITIONS AS POWER (TEXT-DERIVED)

Washington intentionally defines terms before arguing.

From the text:

- **Knowledge**: facts, information, and skills acquired through experience or education
- **Education**: systematic instruction, especially at school or university

The author exposes that although these terms appear synonymous, they function **very differently under control**.

If education is controlled, knowledge becomes limited.
If knowledge is limited, intelligence is manufactured.

III. CORE CLAIMS EMERGING FROM THE TEXT

(Strictly Derived from Chapter 3)

1. Education without knowledge produces compliance
2. Knowledge produces intelligence; intelligence produces discernment
3. Identity is foundational to self-awareness
4. Mainstream SEL models are culturally shallow
5. Generic frameworks erase lived experience
6. Cultural omission creates cognitive dissonance
7. True empowerment begins with knowledge of self

This chapter reframes ignorance not as lack of schooling, but as **misdirected instruction**.

IV. CRITIQUE OF MAINSTREAM SEL (TEXT-FAITHFUL)

Washington introduces Social Emotional Learning not as a rejection, but as a **partial framework**.

The critique is precise:

- SEL emphasizes behavior management
- SEL avoids identity
- SEL generalizes adolescence
- SEL ignores cultural specificity

Without identity, self-awareness collapses.
Without self-awareness, SEL becomes behavioral compliance.

This is not theoretical critique.
It is experiential analysis.

V. KNOWLEDGE OF S.E.L.F. AS CORRECTIVE

Washington positions **Knowledge of S.E.L.F.** as an intentional alternative, not a supplement.

The framework:

- centers identity
- names culture explicitly
- confronts cognitive dissonance
- empowers articulation of self

The example lesson *Love Yourself (The Skin You're In)* illustrates how:

- language shapes identity
- naming disrupts insecurity
- knowledge produces confidence

This is education **in service of intelligence**, not obedience.

VI. SEMINAR QUESTIONS (COLLEGIATE LEVEL)

These questions demand **definition-based reasoning**.

1. Why does Washington insist on defining knowledge and education separately?
2. How does control of education lead to miseducation?
3. Why is identity essential to self-awareness?
4. How does cognitive dissonance function as a defense mechanism?
5. Why does Washington argue that mainstream SEL misses its target audience?
6. How does Knowledge of S.E.L.F. restore intellectual agency?
7. Why is knowledge framed as power rather than information?

Students must cite **specific language** from the chapter.

VII. WRITING & RESEARCH EXPECTATIONS (COLLEGIATE)

Analytical Essay

Prompt:
Using Chapter 3 only, analyze how control of education results in miseducation despite schooling.

Requirements:

- Text-based definitions
- Systemic analysis
- No outside theory
- No anecdotal substitution

Conceptual Argument

Prompt:
Explain why Washington argues that one can be educated and still be enslaved.

VIII. INSTRUCTOR FACILITATION NOTES

- Do not rush definition work
- Push students to interrogate assumptions
- Keep focus on **control**, not intent
- Expect resistance when identity is centered
- Reinforce continuity with Chapters 1 and 2

This chapter often destabilizes students' trust in institutions.
That destabilization is necessary.

IX. KNOWLEDGE OF S.E.L.F. — COLLEGIATE ALIGNMENT

SELF Conscience is fully activated here as:

- awareness of identity
- recognition of cultural erasure
- intellectual courage to redefine self

Knowledge of self is framed as **precondition to liberation**.

X. WHY THIS CHAPTER MATTERS AT THE UNIVERSITY LEVEL

Universities assume:

- education equals knowledge
- credentials equal intelligence

This chapter dismantles that assumption and replaces it with a more dangerous question:

Who benefits from what you are taught to know?

THE MISEDUCATION OF THE NEGRO

IN THE 21ST CENTURY

COLLEGE / UNIVERSITY / PROFESSOR'S EDITION

CHAPTER 4 — CULTURE = INTELLIGENCE = BEHAVIOR

(Environment, Conditioning, and the Manufacturing of Outcomes)

I. ACADEMIC POSITIONING OF THE CHAPTER (FOR FACULTY)

Chapter 4 is not metaphorical.
It is **equational**.

Cedric A. Washington asserts that:

- culture shapes intelligence
- intelligence produces behavior
- behavior is therefore **predictable**, not mysterious

This chapter dismantles dominant narratives that frame behavior as:

- moral failure
- individual deficiency
- genetic inevitability

At the collegiate level, this chapter functions as:

- a **behavioral theory**
- a **cultural indictment**
- a **direct challenge to deficit-based education**
- a **reframing of discipline and accountability**

This chapter should be taught as a **system-level explanation**, not a motivational concept.

II. THE EQUATION AS INTELLECTUAL FRAMEWORK (TEXT-DERIVED)

Washington presents the equation:

Culture = Intelligence = Behavior

This equation asserts:

- Intelligence is not innate in isolation
- Intelligence is shaped by environment and culture
- Behavior is the visible outcome of learned intelligence

Behavior, therefore, is **taught**.

This framework rejects the idea that behavior emerges independent of context.

III. CORE CLAIMS EMERGING FROM THE TEXT

(Strictly Derived from Chapter 4)

From the author's language and sequencing:

1. Culture precedes intelligence
2. Intelligence precedes behavior
3. Environment conditions decision-making
4. Devalued culture produces devalued self-perception
5. Schools misinterpret behavior when culture is ignored
6. Discipline without cultural understanding reinforces miseducation
7. Reprogramming behavior requires reprogramming environment

This chapter reframes behavior as **outcome**, not origin.

IV. HISTORICAL AND IDEOLOGICAL ANCHORING

Washington grounds this chapter through:

- historical conditioning of enslaved Africans
- post-slavery environmental design
- the Willie Lynch Letter as behavioral blueprint
- modern schooling parallels

The argument is not that history *influences* behavior, but that it **engineers it**.

V. INSTITUTIONAL IMPLICATIONS (TEXT-FAITHFUL)

Schools often operate as if:

- culture is irrelevant
- intelligence is neutral
- behavior is choice

Washington exposes this as institutional denial.

When schools:

- ignore culture
- suppress identity
- criminalize expression

They misread behavior and punish intelligence.

VI. SEMINAR QUESTIONS (COLLEGIATE LEVEL)

These questions are designed for **deep analytical engagement**.

1. Why does Washington present culture, intelligence, and behavior as an equation?
2. How does environment shape intelligence according to the chapter?
3. Why is behavior predictable within cultural systems?
4. How does this chapter challenge deficit-based narratives?
5. What role does schooling play in reinforcing behavioral outcomes?
6. Why does discipline fail when culture is ignored?
7. How does this chapter reframe accountability?

Students must ground responses in **explicit textual language**.

VII. INTERDISCIPLINARY APPLICATION

(Without Introducing Outside Theory)

This chapter operates within:

- **Education**: discipline, pedagogy, curriculum
- **Sociology**: social conditioning, environment
- **Psychology**: behavioral development
- **African American Studies**: cultural survival
- **Criminal Justice**: behavior interpretation

Washington collapses these disciplines because lived reality already has.

VIII. WRITING & RESEARCH EXPECTATIONS (COLLEGIATE)

Analytical Essay

Prompt:
Using Chapter 4 only, analyze how Washington's equation reframes behavior as a learned outcome rather than a personal failure.

Requirements:

- Text-based explanation
- System-level reasoning
- No anecdotal substitution
- No outside sources

Applied Analysis

Prompt:
Explain how changing environment can change behavior using Washington's framework.

IX. INSTRUCTOR FACILITATION NOTES

- Do not moralize behavior
- Recenter discussion on **conditioning**
- Expect resistance to environmental explanations
- Avoid genetic determinism arguments
- Reinforce continuity with Chapters 1–3

This chapter often exposes institutional blind spots.

X. KNOWLEDGE OF S.E.L.F. — COLLEGIATE ALIGNMENT

SELF Governing and **Social Conscience** converge here.

Students are pushed to:

- recognize conditioning
- resist internalized narratives
- understand responsibility without blame

Behavior is framed as **modifiable**, not fixed.

XI. WHY THIS CHAPTER MATTERS AT THE UNIVERSITY LEVEL

Universities train:

- educators
- policymakers
- administrators
- psychologists

This chapter challenges them to reconsider:

What they punish
What they reward
What they misunderstand

THE MISEDUCATION OF THE NEGRO

IN THE 21ST CENTURY

COLLEGE / UNIVERSITY / PROFESSOR'S EDITION

CHAPTER 5 — PARENTS AND THE ENVIRONMENT

(Rearing, Accountability, and the Transmission of Intelligence)

I. ACADEMIC POSITIONING OF THE CHAPTER (FOR FACULTY)

Chapter 5 shifts responsibility from **institutions alone** to the **shared custody of development** between parents, community, and environment.

Washington does not absolve systems.
He exposes how **environment completes the work miseducation begins**.

At the collegiate level, this chapter must be treated as:

- a **rearing analysis**
- a **community accountability framework**
- a **behavioral transmission study**
- a **direct confrontation of denial**

This chapter is intentionally uncomfortable because it removes the luxury of blame without ownership.

II. CORE CLAIMS EMERGING FROM THE TEXT

(Strictly Derived from Chapter 5)

From the author's language and progression, the chapter asserts:

1. Intelligence is transmitted through environment
2. Parents are primary carriers of learned behavior
3. Trauma is passed generationally through rearing
4. Absence of accountability produces normalized dysfunction
5. Community silence reinforces miseducation
6. Schools inherit behaviors shaped at home
7. Environment conditions expectations of self

This chapter insists that **misinformed adults raise misinformed children**.

III. REARING AS CULTURAL INTELLIGENCE (TEXT-FAITHFUL)

Washington defines **rearing** as a cultural act.

Rearing determines:

- how children speak
- how they respond to authority
- how they view intelligence
- how they interpret respect

The chapter emphasizes that **what is normalized becomes intelligence**.

Behavior learned at home is not accidental.
It is conditioned.

IV. THE ROLE OF THE BLACK FAMILY (AUTHOR'S FRAMING)

Washington identifies:

- the removal of the Black man from the household
- the overburdening of the Black woman
- the erosion of communal accountability

Not as moral failure—but as **historically engineered outcomes**.

The environment becomes the surrogate parent.

V. ENVIRONMENT AS A TEACHER

According to the chapter, environment teaches:

- survival over stability
- reaction over reflection
- defense over vulnerability
- performance over preparation

This intelligence is **functional**, not defective.

The tragedy lies in punishing students for mastering what their environment demanded.

VI. SEMINAR QUESTIONS (COLLEGIATE LEVEL)

Designed for sustained, graduate-level discourse.

1. How does Washington define rearing within cultural context?
2. Why does environment function as a teacher?
3. How does normalized dysfunction become intelligence?
4. Why are schools unprepared to address home-taught behaviors?
5. How does community silence perpetuate miseducation?
6. Why does Washington insist on accountability without condemnation?
7. How does this chapter complicate traditional narratives of blame?

Students must cite **language from the chapter directly**.

VII. INSTITUTIONAL CONSEQUENCES

When schools ignore environment:

- discipline becomes punishment
- intervention becomes reaction
- curriculum becomes irrelevant

Washington argues that **schools do not correct environment—they collide with it**.

VIII. WRITING & RESEARCH EXPECTATIONS (COLLEGIATE)

Analytical Essay

Prompt:
Using Chapter 5 only, analyze how Washington connects rearing, environment, and behavior.

Requirements:

- Text-based evidence
- System-level analysis
- No external theorists
- No anecdotal substitution

Reflective Analysis (Academic Tone)

Prompt:
Explain how miseducation continues through parental normalization rather than institutional policy alone.

IX. INSTRUCTOR FACILITATION NOTES

- Avoid parent-blaming language
- Maintain structural analysis
- Redirect emotional responses toward accountability
- Reinforce continuity with Chapters 1–4
- Emphasize **shared custody of development**

This chapter often forces students to confront inherited intelligence.

X. KNOWLEDGE OF S.E.L.F. — COLLEGIATE ALIGNMENT

SELF Conscience and **Social Conscience** intersect here.

Students are guided to:

- identify inherited behavior
- understand conditioning without shame
- recognize responsibility without denial

Rearing becomes the bridge between culture and behavior.

XI. WHY THIS CHAPTER MATTERS AT THE UNIVERSITY LEVEL

Universities produce:

- educators
- counselors
- social workers
- policymakers

This chapter demands they ask:

What intelligence did this environment require?

Until that question is answered, intervention remains incomplete.

THE MISEDUCATION OF THE NEGRO

IN THE 21ST CENTURY

COLLEGE / UNIVERSITY / PROFESSOR'S EDITION

CHAPTER 6 — HIP-HOP

(Culture, Consciousness, and the Commodification of Trauma)

I. ACADEMIC POSITIONING OF THE CHAPTER (FOR FACULTY)

Chapter 6 functions as a **cultural indictment** and a **consciousness call**.

Washington does not treat Hip-Hop as entertainment alone.
He frames it as:

- a cultural transmitter
- a behavioral influencer
- a globalized commodity
- a battleground for control of narrative

At the college level, this chapter must be treated as:

- a **cultural studies text**
- a **media literacy critique**
- a **political economy analysis**
- a **behavioral conditioning case study**

This chapter sits at the intersection of **culture = intelligence = behavior**.

II. CORE CLAIMS EMERGING FROM THE TEXT

From the author's language and sequencing, the chapter asserts:

1. Hip-Hop is an African American culture
2. Music functions as a mood setter and behavioral influence
3. Hip-Hop began as storytelling, not glorification
4. The music industry mirrors slave-master dynamics
5. Intellectual property is extracted from Black creators
6. Certain rap narratives perpetuate self-destructive behavior
7. Cultural control determines cultural outcome

Hip-Hop is not neutral.
It teaches.

III. HIP-HOP AS CULTURAL TRANSMITTER (TEXT-FAITHFUL)

Washington frames Hip-Hop as:

- a reflection of environment
- a megaphone for trauma
- a global export of Black culture

When trauma becomes the most marketable narrative, **pain becomes product**.

This chapter insists that:

Culture that is not protected will be exploited.

IV. THE MUSIC BUSINESS AS MODERN ENSLAVEMENT

Using the author's language and examples, the chapter exposes:

- master and slave terminology
- ownership imbalance
- contractual exploitation
- profit without control

The structure of the music industry mirrors historical oppression by:

- separating creator from ownership
- rewarding performance over consciousness
- monetizing dysfunction

This is not coincidence.
It is design.

V. HOUSE NEGRO VS. FIELD NEGRO — CULTURAL APPLICATION

Washington applies the analogy to Hip-Hop culture:

- **House Negro**: rewarded, protected, privileged, obedient to the system
- **Field Negro**: critical, resistant, community-centered

When artists:

- leave the hood
- profit from trauma
- continue to sell destruction

They occupy a **house position** while the masses remain in the field.

VI. SEMINAR QUESTIONS (COLLEGIATE LEVEL)

Designed for sustained, high-level discourse.

1. How does Washington define Hip-Hop as culture rather than genre?
2. Why is music described as a mood setter?
3. How does the music industry replicate slave dynamics?
4. What responsibility does the artist hold to the community?
5. How does Hip-Hop influence intelligence and behavior?
6. Why does Washington argue Hip-Hop must be protected?
7. How does this chapter connect to Culture = Intelligence = Behavior?

Students must ground responses **directly in chapter language**.

VII. BEHAVIORAL CONSEQUENCES (TEXT-DERIVED)

Washington does not argue that Hip-Hop creates violence alone.
He argues it **reinforces normalized dysfunction**.

Repeated exposure to:

- violence
- misogyny
- hyper-materialism
- nihilism

Conditions intelligence and shapes behavior—especially in environments already under strain.

VIII. WRITING & RESEARCH EXPECTATIONS (COLLEGIATE)

Analytical Essay

Prompt:
Using Chapter 6 only, analyze how Hip-Hop functions as both cultural expression and behavioral conditioning.

Requirements:

- Text-based evidence
- Cultural analysis
- No external theorists
- No anecdotal substitution

Media Critique

Prompt:
Explain how control of narrative determines cultural outcome in Hip-Hop.

IX. INSTRUCTOR FACILITATION NOTES

- Do not dismiss Hip-Hop as "just music"
- Avoid moral panic language
- Keep focus on **systems of control**
- Allow discomfort without deflection
- Reinforce continuity with Chapters 4 and 5

This chapter often provokes defensiveness—stay anchored in text.

X. KNOWLEDGE OF S.E.L.F. — COLLEGIATE ALIGNMENT

Social Conscience and **Aspirations** intersect here.

Students are guided to:

- recognize cultural influence
- question consumption patterns
- understand responsibility tied to platform

Culture is power when it is **conscious**.

XI. WHY THIS CHAPTER MATTERS AT THE UNIVERSITY LEVEL

Universities teach:

- media literacy
- cultural theory
- communication
- social influence

This chapter forces students to ask:

Who controls what we consume—and why?

THE MISEDUCATION OF THE NEGRO

IN THE 21ST CENTURY

COLLEGE / UNIVERSITY / PROFESSOR'S EDITION

CHAPTER 7 — POLITICS

(Power, Voting, and the Illusion of Representation)

I. ACADEMIC POSITIONING OF THE CHAPTER (FOR FACULTY)

Chapter 7 exposes politics as **performance without resolution** for the so-called African American.

Washington does not treat politics as civic engagement alone.
He presents it as:

- a cycle of dependency
- a redistribution of hope without repair
- a system that absorbs Black participation while preserving imbalance

At the college level, this chapter must be treated as:

- a **political literacy intervention**
- a **historical continuity analysis**
- a **critique of partisan loyalty**
- a **study of power without agenda**

This chapter confronts students with a fundamental question:
What has political participation actually produced?

II. CORE CLAIMS EMERGING FROM THE TEXT

From the author's language and sequencing, the chapter asserts:

1. Political parties court Black votes without delivering structural change
2. Voting has not resolved issues of opportunity, employment, and justice
3. Representation does not equal empowerment
4. Political allegiance substitutes for collective agenda
5. Black participation is essential to electoral victory
6. Black outcomes remain unchanged across administrations
7. Power is not granted—it is organized

Politics is framed as **cyclical engagement without resolution**.

III. HISTORICAL CONTINUITY OF POLITICAL MISINFORMATION

Washington situates Black political engagement within:

- post-Civil War exclusion
- Jim Crow suppression
- delayed voting rights
- modern party alignment

Despite access to the ballot, outcomes remain consistent.

The chapter asserts that **access without agenda is control**.

IV. DEMOCRAT, REPUBLICAN, AND THE BLACK VOTE (TEXT-FAITHFUL)

Washington does not endorse a party.
He interrogates **both**.

The recurring pattern:

- Black votes are mobilized
- Elections are won
- Structural conditions remain

The phrase "opportunities, employment, and justice" remains unresolved across administrations.

This repetition is intentional.

V. POLITICAL THEATER VS. COMMUNITY POWER

Washington distinguishes:

- participation from power
- symbolism from substance
- visibility from control

Political enthusiasm without economic and cultural organization becomes ritual.

The chapter insists:

Voting alone does not constitute liberation.

VI. SEMINAR QUESTIONS (COLLEGIATE LEVEL)

Designed for extended political analysis and discourse.

1. Why does Washington argue that political participation has not produced liberation?
2. How does the Black vote function electorally versus structurally?
3. Why are opportunities, employment, and justice recurring demands?
4. What is the difference between representation and power?
5. How does partisan loyalty suppress collective agenda?
6. Why does Washington reject reliance on either political party?
7. What would organized political power require beyond voting?

All responses must be anchored in **chapter language**.

VII. INSTITUTIONAL ILLUSION OF PROGRESS

Washington critiques:

- symbolic milestones
- historic "firsts"
- representation narratives

Without structural ownership, milestones do not transform lived reality.

The chapter reframes progress as **measurable outcomes**, not symbolic events.

VIII. WRITING & RESEARCH EXPECTATIONS (COLLEGIATE)

Analytical Essay

Prompt:
Using Chapter 7 only, analyze how Washington critiques political participation without agenda.

Requirements:

- Text-based analysis
- Historical continuity
- No external political theorists
- No partisan framing

Position Paper

Prompt:
Explain why Washington argues that voting without organization sustains miseducation.

IX. INSTRUCTOR FACILITATION NOTES

- Avoid partisan debate
- Recenter discussion on **outcomes**
- Emphasize continuity with Chapters 1–6

- Expect discomfort around civic identity
- Maintain structural focus

This chapter often destabilizes students' assumptions about democracy.

X. KNOWLEDGE OF S.E.L.F. — COLLEGIATE ALIGNMENT

Aspirations and **Social Conscience** converge here.

Students are guided to:

- distinguish participation from power
- recognize economic and cultural leverage
- understand political agency beyond ballots

Power is collective, not ceremonial.

XI. WHY THIS CHAPTER MATTERS AT THE UNIVERSITY LEVEL

Universities produce:

- voters
- policymakers
- analysts
- organizers

This chapter demands they ask:

Who benefits from my participation?

Until that question is answered, civic engagement remains incomplete.

THE MISEDUCATION OF THE NEGRO

IN THE 21ST CENTURY

COLLEGE / UNIVERSITY / PROFESSOR'S EDITION

CHAPTER 9 — REVELATION

(Four Hundred Years Are Up)

I. ACADEMIC POSITIONING OF THE FINAL CHAPTER

Chapter 9 is not a conclusion — it is a **reckoning**.

At the college and university level, this chapter functions as:

- a **capstone ideological synthesis**
- a **historical verdict**
- a **theological exposure**
- a **call to intellectual awakening**

Washington transitions from diagnosis to **revelation**, grounding his argument in:

- research methodology
- biblical text
- historical continuity
- modern global events

This chapter demands **intellectual courage**, not agreement.

II. DEFINING "MISEDUCATION" (TEXT-BASED)

Washington anchors the chapter by defining miseducation as:

poor, wrong, or harmful education.

From the text, miseducation includes:

- false origin narratives
- erased pre-slavery history
- controlled religious interpretation
- political dependency
- identity confusion
- institutional silence

Miseducation is not accidental — it is **systemic**.

III. EDUCATION VS. KNOWLEDGE — FINAL DISTINCTION

Washington reasserts the central thesis:

- Education = instruction
- Knowledge = understanding + experience

Education without knowledge produces:

- compliance
- credentialed confusion
- obedience without consciousness

This distinction frames the entire chapter.

IV. THE BIBLE AS HISTORY, NOT METAPHOR

Washington situates the Bible as:

- a historical document
- a cultural archive
- a suppressed origin record

Key assertions derived directly from the text:

- African American history does not begin with slavery
- Pre-slavery history exists in the Old Testament
- Separation of church and state prevents historical clarity
- Interpretation replaces instruction

The Bible becomes a **contested site of truth**.

V. DEUTERONOMY 28 AND HISTORICAL CONTINUITY

Washington positions Deuteronomy 28 as:

- prophecy
- warning
- lived reality

Themes include:

- captivity
- scattering
- loss of language
- loss of culture
- forced worship
- psychological bondage

This framing connects:

- scripture
- transatlantic slavery
- modern African American identity

VI. POLITICS, RELIGION, AND CONTROL

The chapter identifies politics as:

- manipulative
- partisan
- disconnected from Black liberation

Washington asserts:

- Democrats and Republicans do not resolve Black agendas
- Voting has not yielded structural change
- Power is misdirected through dependency

The Black vote becomes leverage without ownership.

VII. THE 400-YEAR MARK AND GLOBAL DISRUPTION

Washington marks:

- 1619 → 2019
- slavery → pandemic

COVID-19 becomes:

- global pause
- institutional exposure
- spiritual disruption

Churches closed.
Systems stalled.
Reality surfaced.

This moment is framed as **revelatory**, not coincidental.

VIII. REVELATION — ACADEMIC DEFINITION (TEXT-ALIGNED)

Revelation is defined as:

- sudden awareness
- divine disclosure
- historical exposure
- undeniable truth

Washington reframes Revelation as:

- intellectual awakening
- identity recovery
- consciousness shift

Not apocalypse — **recognition**.

IX. CULTURE = INTELLIGENCE = BEHAVIOR (FINAL SYNTHESIS)

The trilogy completes itself.

Culture shapes:

- intelligence

Intelligence shapes:

- behavior

Behavior sustains:

- systems

Until culture is reclaimed, miseducation persists.

X. SEMINAR QUESTIONS (CAPSTONE LEVEL)

1. How does Washington define revelation differently from religion?
2. Why is pre-slavery history essential to disrupting miseducation?
3. How does separation of church and state maintain confusion?
4. Why has political participation not produced liberation?
5. How does COVID-19 function symbolically in the text?
6. What does Washington mean by "chosen people"?
7. Why must revelation precede transformation?

Responses must remain **strictly text-derived**.

XI. COLLEGIATE WRITING REQUIREMENTS

Capstone Analytical Paper

Prompt:
Using Chapter 9 only, analyze how revelation functions as an intellectual, spiritual, and political awakening in *The Miseducation of the Negro in the 21st Century*.

Requirements:

- Textual evidence
- Historical alignment
- No external reinterpretation
- No theological defense

Reflective Synthesis Essay

Prompt:
Explain how Washington connects miseducation, religion, politics, and global crisis into a single framework of revelation.

XII. KNOWLEDGE OF S.E.L.F. — FINAL ALIGNMENT

This chapter activates **all five SELF Mastery Areas**:

- SELF Conscience
- SELF Governing
- Social Conscience
- Aspirations
- Good People Skills

Revelation is the gateway to **SELF mastery**.

XIII. WHY THIS CHAPTER BELONGS IN HIGHER EDUCATION

Universities claim to teach:

- critical thinking

- research
- truth

This chapter tests that claim.

It asks:

What happens when education confronts its own origin story?

XIV. FINAL DECLARATION (TEXT-FAITHFUL)

Washington closes not with apology, but affirmation:

I AM a trailblazer.
I AM destined to succeed.
Speak it. Believe it. Do it.

This is not motivational rhetoric.
It is **intellectual inheritance**.

APPENDICES

COLLEGE / UNIVERSITY / PROFESSOR'S EDITION

APPENDIX A

AUTHOR'S PEDAGOGICAL POSITION (COLLEGIATE CONTEXT)

This text is not written to persuade agreement.
It is written to **force examination**.

The instructional posture of *The Miseducation of the Negro in the 21st Century* at the college level is grounded in:

- text-based analysis
- historical interrogation
- identity examination
- institutional critique

Students are expected to **engage**, not comply.

Discomfort is not a flaw in learning — it is evidence of cognitive engagement.

APPENDIX B

VOCABULARY SOURCE DECLARATION (TEXT-DERIVED ONLY)

All academic vocabulary used throughout the Teacher's Edition and Student Workbook is **intentionally drawn from the author's text**, including but not limited to:

- miseducation
- privilege
- figurehead
- knowledge
- education
- culture
- intelligence
- behavior
- cognitive dissonance
- identity
- environment
- rearing
- oppression
- liberation
- revelation
- conscience
- empowerment

No substitute language is permitted.
Definitions must reflect **contextual usage**, not dictionary replacement.

APPENDIX C

COURSE IMPLEMENTATION MODELS (COLLEGE)

This text may be implemented as:

Option 1:
African American Studies (Upper Division)

Option 2:
Education / Teacher Preparation Program

Option 3:
Sociology / Cultural Studies

Option 4:
Religion, Ethics, or Philosophy Seminar

Option 5:
Interdisciplinary Capstone Course

Each model maintains:

- chapter-by-chapter sequencing
- seminar-based discussion
- text-grounded assessment

APPENDIX D

SEMINAR DISCUSSION NORMS

To protect academic rigor and student safety:

1. Arguments must cite the text
2. Personal attacks are prohibited
3. Faith may be discussed, not defended
4. Politics may be analyzed, not campaigned
5. Identity discussions require respect
6. Silence is permitted
7. Growth is expected

APPENDIX E

WRITING STANDARDS & EXPECTATIONS

All written work must demonstrate:

- direct textual evidence
- clear thesis formation
- alignment to chapter themes
- academic tone
- original analysis

Unsupported opinion ≠ analysis.

APPENDIX F

ASSESSMENT ALIGNMENT (COLLEGIATE)

Formative Assessments

- seminar participation
- reflection journals
- chapter critiques

Summative Assessments

- analytical essays
- synthesis papers
- capstone projects

Grades reflect **depth of engagement**, not agreement.

APPENDIX G

KNOWLEDGE OF S.E.L.F. — HIGHER EDUCATION ALIGNMENT

The Knowledge of S.E.L.F. (Social Empowerment Learning Framework) operates as the **SEL spine** of the text:

1. SELF Conscience
2. SELF Governing
3. Social Conscience
4. Aspirations
5. Good People Skills

At the collegiate level, these are **examined**, not simplified.

APPENDIX H

FACULTY DISCLAIMER (ACADEMIC FREEDOM)

This text:

- does not mandate belief
- does not require ideology
- does not replace institutional doctrine

It exists to:

- provoke thought
- examine systems
- restore agency

Academic freedom is preserved.

APPENDIX I

IMPLEMENTATION CAUTION

This work challenges:

- institutional comfort
- traditional narratives
- inherited assumptions

Faculty should prepare for:

- resistance
- emotional response
- ideological tension

These are **expected outcomes** of critical education.

APPENDIX J

AUTHOR'S FINAL INSTRUCTION TO THE READER

When you know better, you must do better.
Knowledge without action sustains miseducation.
Education without consciousness sustains slavery.

This text is a mirror.

www.ingramcontent.com/pod-product-compliance
Lightning Source LLC
Chambersburg PA
CBHW041611260326
41914CB00012B/1459